The Mysterious Rules:

Tips for Kick-starting Your Career

DISCLAIMER

Copyright © by H. HOYLES 2022. All rights reserved.

Before this document is duplicated or reproduced in any manner, the publisher's consent must be gained. Therefore, the contents within can neither be stored electronically, transferred, nor kept in a database. Neither in Part nor full can the document be copied, scanned, faxed, or retained without approval from the publisher or creator.

TABLE OF CONTENTS

DISCLAIMER	1
TABLE OF CONTENTS	3
INTRODUCTION	5
Chapter 1	8
THE MYSTERIOUS RULES	8
competency, commitment, and compatibility	8
Chapter 2	16
Getting Started Mysteries	16
Chapter 3	20
The Mysteries of Changing Others' Perceptions	20
Recognize Your Storytelling Style	20
Chapter 4	31
Mysteries of completing the task	31

INTRODUCTION

This book offers readers far more than just suggestions for starting their careers; it can benefit everyone from interns to CEOs.

You've been hired. What's next?

Nobody instructs you on how to behave on your first day in a new position. Nobody instructs you on how to accept responsibility, control expectations, or deal with office politics. Nobody tells you how to advance in a company.

The unspoken rules—the specific methods of doing things that supervisors require but do not explain and that top performers do but are unaware of—hold the solutions to these professional unknowns.

The issue is that schools don't teach these laws. Instead, they are shared over meals or by mentors with their mentees, resulting in an unequal playing field where the insiders prosper while the outsiders struggle via trial and error.

Before now.

H. HOYLES demystifies the unwritten laws of labor in this helpful manual. The book offers practical advice you can use right now for your circumstance and will guide you through unavoidable queries like:

How do I manage my time when my priorities conflict?

How can I create connections when working remotely?

How can I ask for assistance without coming out as clumsy or inept?

The only book you need to perform at your peak, distinguish yourself from your colleagues, and position yourself for a rewarding career is The Unspoken Rules.

Chapter 1

THE MYSTERIOUS RULES

competency, commitment, and compatibility

Competence

A person's ability to utilize their training, skills, knowledge, and experience to complete a task is referred to as their level of competence. Competence can also be impacted by additional elements including attitude and physical prowess.

When doing your risk assessments, as an employer, you should take into account the relevant employees' competency. This will assist you in determining the quantity and quality of information, training, education, and supervision that you should offer.

Competence in health and safety ought to be considered an integral part of job operations rather than an extra or afterthought.

You must ensure that contractors are knowledgeable if you utilize them.

Competence just needs to be appropriate to a person's job and place of work

Relevance to the job is the core of expertise. What is essential is that both hazards with frequent occurrences and those with major repercussions are given the necessary attention.

Every director, manager, and employee must possess the competence to identify risks in operational operations and implement the appropriate controls and management strategies.

competent individual

To fulfill your health and safety obligations as an employer, you must choose a "competent person."

A competent individual goes beyond merely having the skills necessary to complete a task safely. A competent individual is someone who, in general, possesses the knowledge, abilities, and experience required to manage health and safety.

A competent entrepreneur

Entrepreneurs with strong skills are better able to make choices that will affect their profitability and satisfy their workforce. Entrepreneurs must be able to turn ideas and chances into action by managing resources if micro enterprises are to attain greater profitability and pleased employees.

Deception, dedication, mechanism, and adaptability are all definitions of commitment.

Dedicating oneself to someone or a cause is the act of committing.

When you accept a job, both you and your employer commit to performing the work satisfactorily and showing up on time.

Work dedication is vital for several reasons. One of the most crucial factors is that it enables a business to achieve its objectives and adhere to its vision. Without a motivated staff, a company risks losing all they have worked so hard to gain over the years, including market share and respect.

Although it is a serious issue, firms may boost dedication at work by making their people feel appreciated. But without a group of enthusiastic and dedicated workers, a company may be in danger.

Workplace commitment increases productivity. Imagine a workplace where people are not dedicated to their work; the results would be disastrous! Such workers frequently utilize their downtime at work to browse the internet for fun or to hunt for new employment prospects. Simply put, this is a waste of time and money.

An organization's ideal comes true when it has a dedicated team of workers. For an organization's or any business's long-term success, a dedicated team of employees is preferable. Building such a culture within the company is the responsibility of the leaders.

Committed workers need a manager who will guide them; they do not need someone who must continually be in their way to do the job. Increased productivity at work is the outcome of such corporate dedication. A compliant team will establish its tasks and make sure they are carried out. They will perform the essential tasks and even more when they arrive at work on time.

Working with commitment adds value by actively participating in topics about the organization. Committed workers bring excellent ideas to the table and are always willing to assist others in seeing those ideas through. To accomplish its objectives, a company requires the commitment and devotion of its personnel.

Compatibility

Making others feel at ease and eager to be around you without coming across as fake or trying too hard is what compatibility entails. This means avoiding undershooting to the point where you appear meek and not overshooting to the point where you appear cocky.

Work compatibility and indicators of human performance are intimately correlated. The idea is that human performance measurements (such as fewer accidents, injuries, and illnesses, and higher work productivity and quality) are better the higher the working compatibility.

Workplace harmony is crucial to ensuring that your business operations function smoothly and reduce turnover rates. Ten percent of employees who quit their employment do so due to disagreements with their coworkers.

It's easier said than done to assemble a team with people that get along. For one thing, it can be challenging to pin down exactly what makes members of a team click with one another. If you ask a highly effective team what helps them function so effectively as a unit, you'll probably hear a variety of different replies. What works for them may not, furthermore, work for other teams.

What do you then? Workplace harmony is crucial to ensuring that your business operations function smoothly and reduce turnover rates. Ten percent of employees who quit their employment do so due to disagreements with their coworkers. When team members go, production declines as a result of a decline in work morale.

Here are three questions you must ask yourself before hiring new employees to make sure they will get along with your current workforce.

Are They Compatible Personalities?

Do They Share the Same Values?

Do Their Motives Align?

Chapter 2
Getting Started Mysteries

Present Yourself as a High Achiever

High-performing workers succeed in their aims and advance the organizations for which they work. They are seen as trustworthy, knowledgeable, and capable by others. How to become a top-performing employee may be of interest to you if you're trying to advance your career and want to be seen as a valuable asset.

Be Proactive

The capacity to take action in advance of an occurrence to guarantee you have full control is known as proactivity. Reactivity, which is when you only react to events after they have occurred, is what it is opposed to.

The proactive person accepts responsibility for their development. A person may choose their life path; external influences do not dictate it. Both positive and negative outcomes are not arbitrarily assigned to outside factors. Instead, the proactive person accepts reality and, in the event of unpleasant occurrences, takes a balanced perspective of both self and other blame. However, it's important to distinguish between two types of accountability: accountability for the past and accountability for bringing about change. This is where the latter is most important. Regardless of whether they were brought on by themselves or others, the proactive person concentrates on finding solutions to issues.

Proactivity in business

Anticipating needs and obstacles will help you and your team be ready to meet them. This is what proactive management entails. It's difficult to foresee every situation. No company or leader can constantly be proactive.

It also implies:

Foresight. preparing for any foreseeable business issues. Suppose you have a year's worth of runway and are a startup. Six months in, not eleven, the proactive management begins seeking out fresh financiers and money.

Opportunism. Unless the manager is proactive enough to look for them, there is always an odd alliance, a new opportunity to add value, or generate more money right around the corner.

Risk Control. Is there a danger that this choice may turn out badly shortly, wonders the proactive manager. If so, the management implements safety measures that would be useful if something went wrong.

Chapter 3

The Mysteries of Changing Others' Perceptions

Recognize Your Storytelling Style

Creating a Good Story Effectively

Pick a strong primary thesis. A great narrative typically builds up to a key moral or message.

Accept conflict...

Have an evident framework.

delve into your individual experiences.

Engage them in conversation.

Watch good storytellers in action.

Limit the scope of your narrative.

Wear good appearance

A confident physical appearance is a quick, efficient technique to increase self-confidence and get rid of acceptance or ability concerns. When you come across as well-groomed, genuinely genuine, and suited for the situation, you feel more at ease, capable, competent, cooperative, and effective.

Image management is the constant practice of assessing and managing how your look affects people and how they react to you. Anyone who has ever needed to improve their self-image, self-esteem, self-confidence, competency, or credibility may benefit from understanding image management. Anyone who has ever wished to persuade someone else, sway opinion or prod them into doing an action—whether at home, at school, in a church, in a community, or at work—can use this advice. It is constructing an accurate, pertinent, alluring, and reasonably priced picture. The success of any type requires intelligence, education, aptitude, initiative, and hard work, but regardless of your age, job, or objective, constant image management may help.

1. HOW YOU ARE DRESSED AND GROOMED IMPACTS HOW YOU THINK.

You can't afford to think poorly of yourself because of a physical characteristic. You feel better about yourself, the circumstance, and other people when you present yourself as genuine, appealing, and acceptable.

2. HOW YOU LOOK AND FEEL IS A DIRECT RESULT OF YOUR CLOTHING.

You can't afford to be unhappy, unproductive, uneasy, hostile, argumentative, inferior, or filled with self-doubt. A confident physical appearance is a quick, efficient technique to increase self-confidence and get rid of acceptance or ability concerns. You feel more at ease, confident, capable, cooperative, and productive when you look presentable, authentically you, and appropriate for the situation.

3. HOW YOU DRESS AND LOOK AFFECTS HOW YOU ACT OR BEHAVE.

You must avoid being uncomfortable, insecure, servile, inappropriate, or out of place. You also cannot act in a defensive, belligerent, cocky, hostile, affectation, superior, or egotistical manner. One of the best strategies for changing behavior and raising performance or productivity levels is to look good.

You act more confidently, at ease, formally, competently, and naturally able to perform at your best when you are well-groomed, appropriately attired for the situation, and personally authentic.

4. HOW YOU ARE DRESSED AND APPEAR AFFECTS HOW PEOPLE REACT TO YOU.

The one aspect of you that is immediately seen and approachable to people is your look. You cannot conceal it.

Your outward appearance conveys a lot about your character, beliefs, attitudes, interests, knowledge, skills, duties, and objectives. Being perceived as disrespectful, hostile, pompous, disorganized, reckless, inept, or unproductive is something you cannot afford. You can't afford to give the wrong impression or put people off by having an unsightly, unsuitable, annoying, or insulting appearance.

You make a good impression and people are more likely to see your great qualities and see you positively when you are well-groomed, appropriately dressed for the occasion, and personally authentic.

One situational element that you can often manage is your look. Although there isn't a single, ideal way to dress, the phrases "genuine," "suitable," "beautiful," and "cheap" are good guidelines. It is crucial to choose and coordinate your outfits tastefully, paying close attention to fit and maintenance. If you want to achieve your goals and objectives, put your appearance and financial situation last and go on.

Consider clothing in a way that is true to who you are as a person—to your personality, beliefs, attitudes, and hobbies. Consider how you should dress for the crowd, the event, and the job at hand. Consider how you would want to present your physical physique in clothing.

Applying the same approach to your grooming. To make a good first and lasting impression about yourself and your talents, learn to handle your wardrobe and grooming aids as a resource, a tool to help you Imagine, feel, and behave as professionally or personally as possible.

I'm challenging you to pay more attention to how your appearance and grooming impact your thinking faculty, how you feel, how you behave, and how other people view you. You can develop a look that is reasonable, appealing, authentic, appropriate, and acceptable for both you and the situation or expectations of others with some thought and practice. This look will assist you in achieving your goals and objectives. Make use of the power of your beauty!

Send the Correct Signals

"When interacting virtually, effective presenting skills are essential. These abilities are even more crucial when there are cultural or linguistic differences on a worldwide scale."

Being here now

the capacity to be totally present and adaptable enough to deal with the unexpected

Honor their time. Start and finish on time. People can stay focused and develop trust if meetings are brief (45 minutes is never a bad thing) and on time.

Be mindful. Disconnect from everything and pay attention. Pay attention to nonverbal indicators that might indicate how individuals are feeling about the subject at hand to determine who is participating and who isn't.

Even when we are delivering content that has been practiced, nerves or distractions might come upon us. Before you begin to "prepare" to give your message, take a deep belly breath.

Making Contact

The capacity to establish connections via empathetic listening and genuine dialogue.

Check-in. Spend some time developing relationships with workers before getting down to business, which, per a recent poll, is one of the biggest problems the virtual team has.

Send invitations cautiously. Does everyone in India or London get up early for the conference call every time? Establish a rule allowing team members to alternate joining global calls outside of business hours once every three months.

Make research. Learn about the regional celebrations, customs, and cultural and technical standards of your international colleagues to have a deeper understanding of the context in which they operate.

Be enquiring. To better grasp what your international colleagues are working on and wanting from you, ask questions and pay attention to the responses. It seems obvious, yet we frequently assume!

Employ video. Use Skype or other video-capable software whenever you can. Employee engagement and reading nonverbal signs will both benefit from this.

Expressive

the capacity to convey one consistent message while effectively expressing sentiments and emotions through speech, body language, voice, and face.

Small nibbles should be given. By pausing often, you can make sure everyone understands.

Add images. A picture does say a thousand words. Where you can, include images to make the material easier to understand.

When using metaphors, be careful. The language-to-language translation is not always accurate. Only your Massachusetts locals would understand you if pieces of a project fit together like peanut butter and fluffy.

Talk loudly. It might be challenging to comprehend what people are saying, whether it's because of a shaky phone connection or a range of dialects. To improve clarity, pronounce your words clearly and stress important topics.

Speed up. How can you comprehend people who speak too quickly? What if they are conversing in a foreign tongue? Always speak more slowly; your listeners will appreciate it.

Self-Knowing

the capacity to accept oneself, to be genuine, and to represent one's ideals in one's choices and deeds.

Recognize your ignorance. It's advisable to research a question's answer if you don't already know the answer. In distant workplaces, rumors may spread quickly on the tiniest bit of false information.

Recognize your prejudices. Bias may make a workplace unworkable. Do you have stereotypes about people from various cultures? If so, what are they? Knowing these ideas exist might help you see misunderstandings and lost chances for more fruitful interactions.

You are adequate. You are your thoughts, and what matters is your intention. Do not let speaking a language other than your own hinder you.

Utilize your advantages. This advice is applicable in all circumstances; become a scientist of your global virtual communications and observe what fosters collaboration and productivity and what undermines it. There are patterns; the key is to recognize them and take advantage of their functions.

It appears to be quite straightforward. Transparent communication is essential for fostering trust and promoting success.

Chapter 4

Mysteries of completing the task

Take Charge

Regardless of your field of employment or job function, it's critical to know how to perform well at work while supporting the demands of your company. To achieve these objectives, one strategy is to assume responsibility at work, which enables you to be more conscious of your place within the overall framework of your firm. You may optimize your contributions to your organization by learning about the significance of work ownership and exercising ownership in the workplace.

Being proactive in your job position and understanding how your job responsibilities contribute to the achievement of overall corporate goals are examples of taking ownership at work. Holding oneself responsible for your effort, regardless of the result, and exhibiting a real interest in assisting the company's success are two other ways to characterize this notion.

Why is it crucial to assume responsibility at work?

Taking initiative at work has several advantages. Here are a few instances:

Keeps you inspired at all times to work hard: Assuming responsibility for your work gives you the freedom to ask questions, come up with ideas, and obtain feedback on your efforts rather than having to wait for your superiors to respond.

Ensures that you match your tasks or initiatives with the objectives of the company: When you take responsibility for your work, you keep open lines of contact with your immediate superior and inquire about the justification for brand-new assignments or job obligations. This enables you to focus your job efforts on achieving organizational goals.

helps you cultivate productive relationships at work: Job ownership helps you do your work while considering how it impacts others and guarantees that you communicate with your superiors to learn more about their expectations since it fosters responsibility and communication with them. Promotes professional growth: Owning your own business motivates you to acquire new skills, take on more responsibilities, and look for new opportunities, all of which may help you advance your career.

strategies to assume responsibility at work

The following is a list of many tactics you might employ to take control at work:

1. Recall the reasons you selected your profession.

You can re-energize yourself for your job responsibilities by reminding yourself of the objectives and professional aspirations that motivated you to apply for and accept a job offer. This is because you are aware of the significance of your work for your life and future career. You may reassess your professional objectives and create tactics for achieving them by recalling why you choose your present work.

This can include developing your interpersonal skills or acquiring additional experience before thinking about internal promotions.

2. Be proactive rather than receptive.

To take control of your work, you must be proactive in carrying out your daily tasks. This includes planning to reduce stress or confusion during hectic workdays, predicting issues and coming up with solutions, seeking clarity on deadlines or assignments, and anticipating difficulties.

3. Work on managing up.

Employees can learn more about their superiors' management styles, communication preferences, and expectations by managing up. Additionally, it motivates staff to have a fruitful working connection with their management. This is a practical method for taking responsibility at work since it enables you to build relationships with your superiors and look for possibilities to advance in experience.

4. Strive to support others' ideas while also expressing your own.

The ability to speak up at team meetings or project-related tasks is a crucial component of taking control of your job. You must have self-assurance and provide evidence for your claims to do this.

However, it's equally crucial to hear the ideas and views of your team as it is to voice your opinions. Experienced staff members and corporate executives frequently provide creative ideas that support organizational objectives. In these circumstances, taking ownership of your work entails respecting other people's opinions and knowing when to assist them by turning their ideas into deeds.

5. Discuss your career goals with your employer.

To take responsibility for your job and reach your professional objectives, You must be open and honest with your manager about your goals for the position, your areas of interest, and the tasks or projects you love the most. They will better understand your needs as an employee if you are honest with them. Additionally, it enables you to define performance benchmarks with your management and choose new duties in line with your interests.

6. Request constructive criticism

Instead of waiting for peer and performance assessments, routinely solicit constructive criticism from your coworkers. You have the opportunity to learn more about how you perform in your role as a colleague and leader by requesting constructive criticism from peers and superiors. It also aids in identifying the areas you should focus on enhancing to assist your business in success.

7. Use active listening techniques

You may utilize active listening to improve your professional communication abilities and take responsibility for your job. It might entail minor verbal gestures and inquiries, as well as non-verbal indicators like nodding, smiling, maintaining eye contact, taking notes, and arranging your body in specific ways.

You may better grasp the demands of your company and your coworkers by actively listening. By keeping your attention on the speaker and taking notes, you can improve your memory. Additionally, being able to actively listen ensures that you understand your job's requirements so that you can carry them out perfectly.

8. Provide problems with solutions

Offering solutions as opposed to only stating concerns is more effective when taking ownership of your job. Take a moment to contemplate how you would resolve a problem on your own before approaching your manager, for instance, if you ran across one. Present the issue during your visit, then quickly provide a few viable remedies you came up with. This demonstrates your initiative and aids in keeping your management informed of workplace events.

9. Improve your awareness of yourself

Understanding your talents, limitations, learning preferences, and personality qualities are known as self-awareness. You can hold yourself responsible, establish objectives for growth, and change the way you operate by having a thorough grasp of your habits and requirements. Create objectives for development and modify your working style to take into account your skills and shortcomings. For instance, you can modify your working style to do activities in certain amounts of time, followed by brief breaks, if you are aware that you have trouble focusing for extended periods.

10. Early on, ask questions.

By raising questions early on in a new project or job assignment, you may take responsibility for your work. It also enables you to ascertain the main goals your boss has set for you as well as the reason for a project or task assignment within your department or the entire business.

11. Offer to take on new responsibilities or team roles

You have the chance to hone your talents and inch closer to career milestones by offering to lead presentations, take on extra work, or transition to a new team function for a project. By forcing you to initiate change rather than waiting for someone else to assign you new tasks and responsibilities, volunteering yourself for these possibilities encourages you to take responsibility for your job.

12. Make the most of opportunities to learn.

Motivating yourself to increase your professional knowledge and working abilities is a crucial component of taking ownership at work. Participating in training programs or certification courses can help you achieve this. You might be able to explore these learning opportunities through your HR department, depending on the business you work for. Otherwise, You can look for certification programs online or in your neighborhood.

13. Identify your professional objectives.

You may target your work efforts toward specified standards and career milestones by setting professional objectives for yourself. This also makes you feel empowered since it encourages you to push your boundaries and offers you a sense of control over your career objectives.

14. Adopt a forward-looking perspective

Always consider how your present actions and habits may affect your coworkers, company, and future career aspirations when accepting responsibility for your job. Consider how your participation in work activities may impact your future skill level and capacity for promotion as one illustration of this.

www.ingramcontent.com/pod-product-compliance
Lightning Source LLC
Chambersburg PA
CBHW050323220526
45465CB00005B/2107